YOUR KNOWLEDGE HAS VALUE

Bibliographic information published by the German National Library:

The German National Library lists this publication in the National Bibliography; detailed bibliographic data are available on the Internet at http://dnb.dnb.de .

Imprint:

Copyright © 2015 GRIN Verlag
Print and binding: Books on Demand GmbH, Norderstedt Germany
ISBN: 9783346088031

This book at GRIN:

https://www.grin.com/document/511928

Anonym

Orfeo's Exile. The Nexus between Emotion and Reason

GRIN Verlag

GRIN - Your knowledge has value

Since its foundation in 1998, GRIN has specialized in publishing academic texts by students, college teachers and other academics as e-book and printed book. The website www.grin.com is an ideal platform for presenting term papers, final papers, scientific essays, dissertations and specialist books.

Visit us on the internet:

http://www.grin.com/

http://www.facebook.com/grincom

http://www.twitter.com/grin_com

Freie Universität Berlin

Department of Philosophy and Humanities

Medieval English Literatures II: Medieval English Literature and the Philosophy of Emotion

Course number: 17331

Summer term 15

Orfeo's Exile- the Nexus between *Emotion* and *Reason*

Table of Contents

1. Introduction

The Middle English romance *Sir Orfeo* is an anonymous poem of the early fourteenth century (1330-40) that has found great resonance with literary research and critique. It has been praised by multiple authors to be a 'small poetic miracle' (Pearsall 1996: 51) or 'one of the most loveliest and charming of all Middle English Romances' (Severs 1961: 187). The romance deals with Orfeo, king of Winchester who fails to save his beautiful wife Eurodis from the underworld and who decides in consequence of this loss to leave his kingdom in order to live in the wilderness. One day he rediscovers Eurodis among sixty ladies, follows her to the underworld, succeeds to bring her back to his kingdom and to restore his power.

The various readings and interpretations of the poem attest its literary relevance among Middle English literary works of art. These readings touch on the work's references to Christian Mythology as well as upon philosophical and psychological questions posed by the authors. For instance Enrico Giaccherini (2002: 4) emphasises the protagonist's decision to go into exile as a reference to Christian mythology. Furthermore, A. C. Spearing provides a psychoanalytic interpretation of the characters according to which Eurodises' behaviour indicates traits of schizophrenia (Spearing 2000: 262-263). Moreover, Peter J. Lucas (1972:1) alludes to the social dimension of the poem. According to Lucas the "testing of social bonds of love and loyalty" depicts the main issue of the poem. Researchers have been inter alia interested in the characters' behaviours and motives for behaving in a certain way in a specific situation. Both Derek Pearsall (1996: 61) and J.K. Knapp point out the "poem's vision of the human condition" (Knapp 1968: 263). According to the former the uniqueness of the poem consists in the way it associates the weakness of human mind and the persistence of human heart (1996:61).

Pearsall indicates the metaphors of "mind" and "heart" in order to allude to the dualism between reason and emotion constituting according to him not only the poem's

1

uniqueness and its core aspect, but also the condition of being human (1996:61). In point of fact, regarded from a retrospective view on humanity's history emotion and reason have been the most distinctive traits in human nature. However, we do not need to go that far in order to recognise the remarkable impact of this dualism on human life, for each decision made by an individual in its everyday life underlies the power of reason and emotion. Thus, can be explained the readers identification with and fascination for the poem. Pearsall does not further illustrate to which extent the forces of 'mind' and the 'heart' at work in the poem are represented in regard to the characters' behaviours. Hence, in compliance with Pearsall's determination, the goal of this paper is first to provide the philosophical medieval[1] notion of *emotion* and *reason* and subsequently to investigate how emotion and reason relate to each other in the poem *Sir Orfeo*.

2. The medieval notion of the *emotion*

Seen from a diachronic perspective, the notion of emotions has undergone different approaches in the field of philosophy and psychology. Recently philosophical interest in emotions has increased due to new findings in other research fields such as cognitive science, developmental and evolutionary psychology, neuroscience and linguistics (Goldie 2010: 2). If we seek to understand how emotions are represented in *Sir Orfeo* as a work of art that mirrors the prevailing world view of its time of emergence, it is crucial to comprehend the medieval notion of emotions. However, even in the Middle Ages different competing conceptions of emotions exist (King 2010:167) offering divergent notions. Still, medieval thinkers were unanimous concerning the inherent qualities of a theory of emotions (King 2010: 167). According to them emotions consist of a cognitive (thought and belief) and a physiological dimension. Yet two occurrences were regarded as completely physiological: the urges and depressions. These occurrences were clearly extracted as being 'purely physiological' (King

---

[1] Looking at the medieval notion of emotion and reason will help us to examine and understand the poem within the historical context it emerged from

2

2010: 167) and contrasted to the so called 'paradigmatic' emotions, such as delight, anger, distress and fear.

Besides philosophical approach, medical and confessional literature provided practical knowledge on emotions during the Middle Ages (King 2010: 168). Many Arabic philosophers who worked as physicians focussed on the medical dimension of emotions. Furthermore, for instance Christian doctrine ascribed an important role to emotions such as compassion and contrition play a fundamental role in Christian thought (King 2010 168). However, among Christian clergy only Christian theologians, who represented the intellectuals of the Middle Ages, were concerned with psychological theories of the emotions.

2.1 Augustine's response to the stoic view of *emotion* and *reason*

The medieval notion of the emotions was fundamentally influenced by Augustine of Hippo's discussions. St. Augustine of Hippo (354-430), who became already as a teenager interested in philosophy and adopted classical teaching to Christian faith, deals with the emotions in his late work *The City of God* (Book 9.4-5 and 14.). In this work Augustine refers to the Stoic view of emotions which indicates that emotions are false and subjective value judgements that stand in contrast to the rational view of reality (Knuuttila 2010: 429). In accordance with the Stoics, Augustine defines emotions as "disturbances" and "mental passions" in *The City of God* (Augustine 1972: 346) and approves to the stoic assumption that emotion oppose to reason. However, he contradicts to the stoic idea that this opposition applies to all emotions (King 2010: 169). According to the theologian emotions can be in obedience to reason. Augustine provides the example of compassion, which he associates to exercising justice and thus to reason (Augustine 1972: 349). Apart from that he disapproves the Stoics, who assume that emotionlessness depicts the ideal state of being. Augustine refers to the Christian doctrine to refute this idea. For instance he emphasises that even Jesus was marked by emotions that were considered to be characteristic for human nature. Moreover, he argues that Christian doctrine invites human beings to feel emotions, such as loving your enemy or fearing God (King 2010: 169).

Besides Augustine underlines the fact that even a wise person may become subject to emotions (Augustine 1972: 346 f.). He gives the example of a Stoic philosopher who was paralysed with fear vis-à-vis a situation, in which a ship he was on was hit by a storm. The story was written by Aulus Gellius, a Latin author, in his work called *Noctes Atticæ*. Gellius had travelled on the shame ship as the Stoic philosopher. When the storm had passed, he as a reasonable man was asked by Gellius why he was paralysed with fear during the storm. In response to this question the stoic philosopher pulls out of his pocket a book written by Epictetus the Greek Stoic philosopher, in which the latter explains that even wise persons are impacted by emotions, underlining, however, that by the force of reason they can overcome their 'disturbances' (Augustine 1972: 346). Gellius who has read the book of the Stoic philosopher points out that according to the Stoics the human soul is unwillingly violated by external objects that provoke emotions such as fear and sadness. These emotional states can yet be overcome by the wise person's power of reason (Augustine 1972: 347). Providing this example Augustine insists that by the force of reason the wise person may overcome his feelings of fear and sadness.

3. Emotion and reason in the romance Sir Orfeo

According to Augustine's exposition emotion and reason cannot be regarded as fundamentally separate concepts. In point of fact, as Augustine maintains, there can be an interplay between them; on the one hand emotions can be in obedience to reason, on the other reason can strengthen a wise person in order to overcome emotions triggered by external objects. On the basis of these assumptions we will in the following examine how emotion and reason are represented in the medieval literary work of art *Sir Orfeo*. In this analysis predominantly the romance's protagonist, King Orfeo, will be at the centre of interest.

3.1 Orfeo's exile- the nexus between *emotion* and *reason*

After King Orfeo fails to rescue his wife Eurodis from the King of fairy, he is in such a way overwhelmed by emotions of sorrow, self-denial and regret that he decides to leave his kingdom and to live in the wilderness.

> The king into his chaumber is go,
> And oft swoned opon the ston,
> And made swiche diol and swiche mon
> That neighe his liif was y-spent -
> Ther was non amendement. (ll. 196-200)
> [...]Into wildernes ichil te
> And live ther evermore
> With wilde bestes in holtes hore;
> And when ye understond that y be spent,
> Make you than a parlement,
> And chese you a newe king. (ll. 212-217)

The aspect of Orfeo's exile has been discussed in several readings. For instance, it has been explained as a sign of 'self-abasement' or 'expiation' (Pearsall 1996: 56). Pearsall regards Orfeo's decision as calculated and as the repetition of his wife's experience. Yet, this does not exclude the fact that the act of abandoning his kingdom and going into the wilderness has emerged from an internal impulse, an emotion. Taking into account the potential consequences of his exile, as for instance the risk of invasion by other powers, it becomes clear that Orfeo's decision is not obedient to reason. Seen from this angle of view, we can assume that he is on the contrary driven by his emotions and not capable of having reasonable thoughts.

His exile depicts the logic consequence of the strength of his emotions, for he is mourning and must move and go on a pilgrimage in order to process his sorrow. The author of the romance alludes to the aspect of pilgrimage by emphasising that Orfeo leaves all his wealth behind, only takes upon himself a pilgrim's mantle and goes barefoot.

5

"Do way!" quath he, "It schal be so!"

Al his kingdom he forsoke;

Bot a sclavin on him he toke.

He no hadde kirtel no hode,

Schert, ne no nother gode,

Bot his harp he tok algate

And dede him barfot out atte gate;

No man most with him go. (ll. 226-233)

However, Orfeo's pilgrimage does not correspond to the common sense of pilgrimage, which ends up in a shrine (Pearsall 1996: 56), it depicts rather an allegory for inner reflection, meditation and the processing of the state of mourning. The author does not indicate to which extent Orfeo is striving for lucidity, still his pilgrimage reveals itself as the process of maturation that results in reasonable behaviour when he follows Eurodice to the world of fairy and frees relieves her from the king of fairy.

Not only pilgrimage but also his harp and the seasons of nature (ll. 257-278) are crucial elements that help him on the one hand to replace his internal dissonance by harmony and on the other guide him on his way to reason.

He toke his harp to him wel right

And harped at his owhen wille.

Into alle the wode the soun gan schille,

That alle the wilde bestes that ther beth

For joie abouten him thai teth,

[…] To here his harping a-fine -

So miche melody was therin; (ll. 270-278)

This passage clearly depicts how Orfeo overcomes his sorrow by playing his harp and lets harmony and joy to revive his soul. Furthermore, Orfeo experiences in the wilderness the cyclical character of the seasons in nature, which serves to him exemplary in order to abandon sorrow and to rediscover hope.

Only after having played on his harp and experienced the seasons in nature Orfeo is able to recognise Eurodis within the sixty ladies riding on horses.

> And on a day he seighe him biside
> Sexti levedis on hors ride (ll. 303-304)
> He aros, and thider gan te.
> To a levedi he was y-come,
> Biheld, and hath wele undernome,
> And seth bi al thing that it is
> His owhen quen, Dam Heurodis.(ll. 318-322)

4. Conclusions

Orfeo's exile depicts emotion and reason as inseparable fundamental pillars of human spirit. The protagonist, representing a wise king who usually behaves according to logic and reasonable motives, is, after having lost his wife, overwhelmed by his emotions. These emotions constitute the breeding soil for his exile. The act of movement (pilgrimage), music and the nature pave the way for Orfeo to rediscover hope and reason. Only after his pilgrimage, Orfeo becomes able to have clear and reasonable thoughts and thus to recognise his wife between the sixty ladies. Even if his decision to leave for exile represents in the first instance an unreasonable decision, we can state that in the end it can be regarded as a necessary condition leading to reasonable behaviour. Moreover, we can assert that Orfeo's reaction to loss and his way to reasoning are typical of the human condition. This aspect allows to the reader to identify with the protagonist and constitutes, thus, the uniqueness of the poem.

5. Works cited

Catholic Online, "St. Augustine of Hippo".

> http://www.catholic.org/saints/saint.php?saint_id=418 (assessed 23-11.2015)

Giaccherini, Enrico, "From *Sir Orfeo* to *Schir Orpheus*: Exile and the Waning of the Middle
Ages", in *Displaced Persons: Conditions of Exile in European Culture*, edited by
Sharon Ouditt (Aldershot: Ashgate, 2002), pp. 1-10.

King Peter, "Emotion in Medieval Thought", in *The Oxford Handbook of Philosophy and
Emotion,* edited by Peter Goldie (Oxford: Oxford University Press, 2010). pp 167-187.

Knapp, J. K., "The Meaning of *Sir Orfeo*", *Modern Language Quarterly 29* (1968), 263-73.

Knuuttila, Simo, "Emotion", in The Cambridge History of Medieval Philosophy, edited by
Robert Pasnau, associate editor Christina van Dyke, 2 vols. (Cambridge: Cambridge
University Press, 2010), vol. 1, pp. 428-40.

Lucas, Peter J., "An Interpretation of *Sir Orfeo*". *Leeds Studies in English 6* (1972), 1-10.

Pearsall, Derek, "Madness in *Sir Orfeo*", in *Romance Reading on the Book: Essays on
Medieval Narrative Presented to Maldwyn Mills*, edited by Jennifer Fellows, Rosalind
Field, Gillian Rogers and Judith Weiss (Cardiff: University of Wales Press, 1996), pp.
51-63.

Saint Augustine, *Concerning The City of God against the Pagans*. trans. Henry Bettenson
with an introduction by John O' Meara. London: Penguin Classics, 1972.

Sir Orfeo, in *The Middle English Breton Lays*, edited by Anne Laskaya and Eve Salisbury,
TEAMS Middle English Texts (Kalamazoo, MI: Medieval Institute Publications,
1995);   http://d.lib.rochester.edu/teams/text/laskaya-and-salisbury-middle-english-
breton-lays-sir-orfeo (assessed on 16-04-2015).

Severs, Burke, "The Anticedents of Sir Orfeo", in *Studies in Medieval Literature in Honor of Professor Albert Croll Baugh*, edited by MacEdward Leach (Philadelphia 1961).